The Further Adventures of
PINOCCHIO
Le Ultime Avventure

Edwin Frank
George Woodman

Your eyes open a crack
to begin with—

The Further Adventures of
PINOCCHIO
Le Ultime Avventure

Poems / Poesie

Edwin Frank

Pictures / Immagini

George Woodman

Lo Specchio d'Arte / New York

Nose in a book

to begin with? What a lie!

Nose in a book of lies,

sniffing out a pack

of lies, nose in a crack,

in the door, the eye spies

in the darkness stories,

    like the one your good father,

who loved marching bands

    and kept regular hours, still tries

to persuade you of. He says

the son will rise tomorrow,

go to school, but you,

you know better than that, the old fool,

let the world go to hell,

I won't miss a single trick.

Featureless as a peeled stick,
I am entirely generic,
aren't I, though my nose
at times may stick
out. But already I forget myself—

Yes, already you forget yourself,
your humble beginnings as a log,
two staring pleading eyes
under a coverlet of bark
in your original sickness.
    Already you forget
who made you in his image—

instead of—I have to interrupt—your own
image more radiant than anyone
or thing, the mirror where all is lost and found.

Take me away, carry me off,
don't bring me back
in your coat pocket, hide me
when everyone else is looking
you don't notice, do you,
intricate, beautiful, and true
like a proof in math, with a perfection
that is equally your bruised
reality, proud flesh
I gaze at like a wall,
a convict scratching his tally,
and still you don't notice at all.

Did I stray? How is it,
    this thing is starting to be,
believe it or not, autobiography?
Dear Diary
entry, forgive me, I was having
the time of my life
before I knew it.
(This is a life?)
I made up a story
I am explaining to you
I am in Beverly Hills in fact
in a hotel looking through
a soiled tatted curtain
    at a back alley at midday.
I am trying to imagine it
    exactly as it is.
I am completely terrified.

It isn't canvas spread
on a stretcher to make a flat
painted landscape for me to play
either the story of my
going to the dogs
or the no less familiar
tale of my reform
(so inevitable, so trite,
each foretold rise and fall)—
no, it's neither
a theatrical
backdrop and definitely not the school
blackboard, this body of truth
where I find myself at loss.

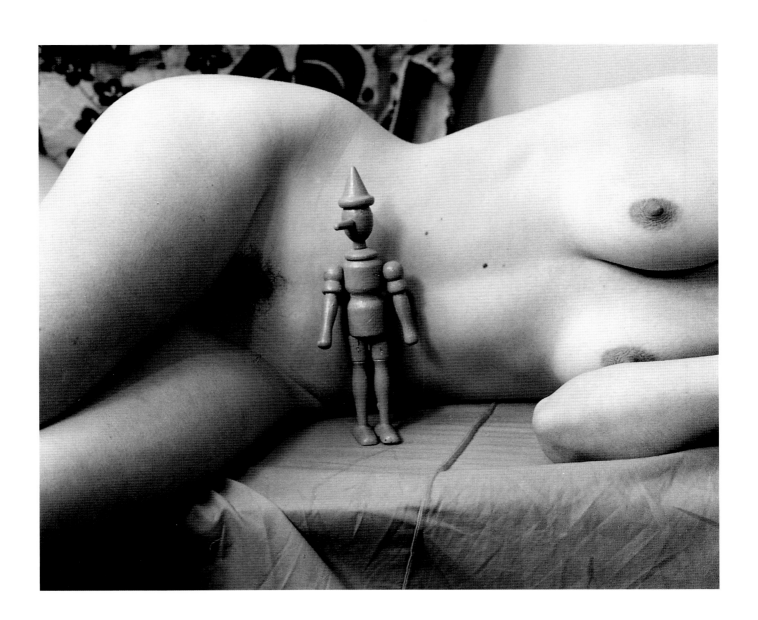

Hitting the books again.
This says, Imagine a pain
which is somebody's, but just where
is it? and who's to say? and what? I swear
there's nothing to it. Only words. Is that clear?
Not that they aren't in pain.
Me too.
Unwitting, I draw the curtain
on the little theater
of never mind. A whole life
I'll never dream of. Who's there?

Mimicry, mockery,
sweet girl, dear boy,
we have a picture of things—
YOU WANT TO ESCAPE FROM THE PICTURE?
YOU THINK YOU CAN TURN YOUR BACK
ON THIS PICTURE? Oh no,
the picture's calling you back,
whether or not you want to listen or see
what's next, yourself led blindfold
   down the gangplank past
those fabled islands
of resemblance in
silence to plunge
into the sea.

Yes, I am going away.

Parenthesis

whose speech is a tree
in flower, whose flesh
is tier after tier
of leaves rising

upward
into her eyes, whose face
shines in shadow
like a waxing moon,

like a waning moon, whose will
is hidden
and at large, shaking
her black hair backward

in the wind, holding
in pale hands her
whole body forward
as a wave—whether

awake or
asleep, dreaming
with open eyes, with eyes
shut, always

I see her,
whose presence is
unbending, a ladder
heavy with symbols

I climb
downward, whose mouth
is made up
once and for all, whose eyes

are two sleepy apples,
whose open
heart is a heartless
chest, whose head a nest

of vipers, who has no head,
who is a mirror shining
all over, whose headless
torso is

a vase, a voice, a flower

Catastrophe,

how did it happen to me,

a total inversion of values?

Eyes open now and watch from any corner.

And what strange company

do I now find myself in?

Bird, baby bear,

ball of string, bottle of linseed oil,

lonely doll—under what unlucky star

    were you born

to puzzle out this fatal hieroglyph?

Who assembled the cast of this crummy play,

mistaking a hero for the prize

    in a Cracker Jack box?

What am I supposed to do with all
these things I call
memories, but which are as unimaginable
as, say, once I was a boy,
now I am a puppet?
Blood, wine—please,
how am I to organize
all these things I wanted
and got and never wanted?
How'd this story become my story—
embarrassingly
repeating itself,
as I do ever more,
mumbler, bumbler, mirror.

Words are fewer now
and far between,
it is not to be expected
    that they will mean
what they say,
so much has gone
unrecognized away
one never had,
if that can be. Today
I met a pilgrim on the road,
who stopped to speak with me.
Pinocchio, he told me, was his name,
    one who had cast off love
yet still had miles to go
before he canceled out a debt
    that he still owed.
He left, and I remained,
    in greater pain.
Like a weathervane, I thought,
from day to day
I turn,
pointing nowhere all at once.

Nose to nose, not quite,

nor eye to eye, and yet

almost looking at

or else

away from each other still

not quite able to tell

are you real, I am a lie,

a real walking talking lie,

but not now, now I

am listening, perhaps

I became real at your first reproach.

/ —

little

cry —

Up in the air as always, out in the open at last,
having shimmied up one strand of Rapunzel's hair
all the way, danced Petrushka's dance,
    that spooky tattoo
his heels beat out on the tin rooftops, run through
every story to every conclusion: you—
luftmensch, loudmouth, lollygagger—
you're done, finished: you can kick away the ladder,
get a final gander from where
you can see it all for what it was and oh
forget it: our shadows running upon the waters
like tears, what can I say?

Pinocchio wishes to thank Alison, Betty,
Christine, Cleopatra, Jessica, Leonora, Saskia and Selva

First Edition
ISBN 0-923183-36-1
Poems © 2004 Edwin Frank
Photographs © 2004 by George Woodman
Published 2004 by
Lo Specchio d'Arte
138 West 17th St. Apt. 4
New York, NY 10011
U.S.A.
Designed by Ilaria Casalino + Fried Rosenstock

Printed and bound in Italy

Distribuzione per l'Italia GLI ORI